THE TWO
PROMISES

THE TWO PROMISES

ROGER FLUTY

ISBN: 978-1-971940-12-0 (sc)
ISBN: 978-1-971940-13-7 (e)

Rev. date: 02/05/2026

CONTENTS

INTRODUCTION

I am not sure how to write a book, but I guess it's a lot like telling a story. My story is one that I hope it will bring Christians together and not have all the boundaries of what I call "Religion has done to our society". I am sure it may be a little controversial, but I hope you read this with an understanding that this truly comes from my heart and more importantly the desire not to let God down. Have you ever had an experience where God has asked you to do something and you have tried to convince yourself that there is no way God would ask you to really do it? Of course, we can look to so many bible stories where a man of God was asked to do something and they tried to run from it. All Jonah had to do was preach a sermon to a city, but it took staying in a whale to get his attention. We all dream of being like Abraham and when he was asked to sacrifice Isaac he simply obeyed and we can see how he was blessed. But I am sure there are more Jonah's out there than Abraham's and I know I would fall into the Jonah camp more often than I would like to admit. I know God has asked me to spread a message through writing a book. I do not think I have read more than three books cover to cover in my life, so asking me to write a book seems very unusual. In fact, I am the one that would tell my daughter to wait and watch the movie "The Lion and the Wardrobe", versus me reading the book with her, which was a school assignment. She read the book cover to cover and when we watched the movie, she was very excited to tell me the book brought the story to life much better than the movie. Did I go and read the book at that time? Of course not, the movie told me enough of the story to satisfy me. So, I am stepping out of my comfort zone in attempting to write a book. If it is successful, then it was only by the grace of God who blessed it. My story is one of looking back over my life and trying to understand why God lead me down the path he has. I feel God has shown me something that he wants me to share in the words of a book. A close friend asked me why I wanted to write a book. If it was something God wanted me to share than I should do it openly and not try and make anything out of it. Those words have stuck with me for almost a year, which has had me trying to get my story out, but again this is how God asked me to do it, and I need to follow his will. This is a story that I fear leaves me without a true religious home, but I will trust God to continue to lead me in the path that he desires.

THE EARLY LIFE

I am like any young American boy with a dream to be successful in life. I look at my teenage years, and I had always had God in my life, and I owe that to my parents who would take me to Sunday school and was a good role model as to what a young boy would vision as a Christian. I can remember my first experience with God when my dad's lounges collapsed. I was barely 5 years old, and I can remember that day like it just happened. It often amazes me; because of how many memories I am already forgetting. As I heard him gasping for breath, I put my hands over my ears and tried to shut it out. I could hear my mom screaming and although you would see that she was panicking she was able to call for help and the ambulance came very fast. My heart was racing as I wanted to shut the noise out, so I walked down into the basement and closed the door. To my surprise our dog Tuffy somehow walked by the door before I closed it and I could even see tears in his eyes. I set down on the steps, and I could hear the men running through the house to get to my dad. At that time, I am not sure how I knew that there was even a God, but I began to pray. I asked God to save my daddy and please do not let him die. I am not sure what happened, but a calm came over me, and I sat on the steps staring out into space while petting Tuffy. I then knew that my daddy would be okay. God heard me that day.

It was 8 years later when I had my next experience with God. I knew I was lost. I would tremble in my bed as I laid down each night, and I would pray to God to please not let me die in my sleep and go to Hell. I have heard about what Hell was like in Sunday school and I knew I did not want to go there. I was not sure how or what it really meant to be saved, but I knew that was the only way to keep from going to that awful place. One night at the church I attended with my parents I knew when the preacher stood in front of the alter and invited all that would come to repentance to come forward, it was meant for me. My legs were trembling and my hands were stuck to the back of the bench so tight you would think they were frozen to it. I finally pried my hands from the bench and walked down the aisle. Wow what a weight that came off me that night. I cried more that night than I thought I had in my whole life, but it was a happy cry. I almost felt like I could fly away. I could not wait to get home to tell my friends what this experience was like. I can remember standing on my porch at dusk with one of my friends. We loved to watch the bats fly around the pole light at the top of our steps leading to the road. There were not many houses on the road where I lived that had a pole light, so this was a big thing to a group of boys. Of course, we all had our BB guns and thought we could shoot the bats. In all those years I do not recall ever hitting one of them. I began to tell my friend about the experience I had at church a few nights earlier. He looked at me and said I was too young at 14 to make that kind of commitment. I said "Why"? Even Jesus was preaching at a younger age than that. He rolled his eyes and said listen, "I plan on having as much fun as I can have and when I turn in my mid 20's I will marry a girl and then I will think about it". That conversation still haunts me today, because my friend got into drugs and other things he should not have and did not live long enough to do what he said he would do. It saddens me to think where he is today. A few days after that my parents told me about baptism, and I was very excited to go down to the creek to be baptized. I told my dad that I want him to be one that helps baptize me and I know it made him feel good. I remember how cold the water was when I first stepped in and the preacher and my dad took me out about waist deep. I know when I came back up out of the water that God was pleased with me, and I felt that calmness come over me again.

I stayed very close to God and participated in the local youth groups and even helped organize a youth rally with two of my close friends, which we had at our local high school football field. There was a huge crowd that showed up and even though I was not part of any of the activities that went on that day, I knew helping put this together was pleasing to God. After I graduated high school, I found myself very confused for the first time in years. My dad was going to help me follow in his footsteps and took me to the coal mines where he worked. I knew that was not for me, so I talked to my parents about going to college instead. I knew money would be an issue, so I agreed to go to the local community college to start out with while I was trying to get accepted in a trade college. I soon found myself following my fleshly desires and you would not see me in church that often. The more I would chase after the worldly things, the less I wanted anything to do with church. I decided to take some time off from college and began working two jobs at a time to support my party life. I finally came to a place where I knew I had strayed so far from God that I was not hearing from him anymore. I met my future wife, and we were friends at that time, but all she talked about was how much she loved God. Her best stories were when she was with her family when they went to church together. They would even have church in her grandmother's house. She wore nothing but skirts and dresses, no make-up, and kept her hair long. Each time I talked with her it would make me miss my relationship I used to have with God. Finally, one night I knew I had enough of the world, and I wanted my God back in my life. I went to church and I went back to the altar and confessed to him and asked his forgiveness. I could not wait to call this girl and tell her the good news. She was so excited for me and finally I asked her out on a date. Of course, the date was to go to church with me. I am not sure how many teenage guys could say that the first date they asked a girl to go on was to go to church, but I could not ask God for a better blessing over this date.

I dated my future wife for almost a year before I asked her to marry me. If she had told me no, we would have both been very disappointed. It was Christmas Eve when I proposed to her and the engagement ring was also her Christmas present. I am sure glad she said yes. Only then did things get a little confusing with my relationship with God. Our favorite date was to go to church with each other, so you would not think it would interfere with my walk with God. I started listening closer to what was being preached at her church, and I noticed it was a little different from what I heard at my church. We know through history that the difference of religious beliefs has caused many wars and separations between groups and even individuals. When I went to the pastor of my church and told him I was confused by some of the things they were saying and doing at her church, his advice was that I should not marry her. He told me, "We would continue to have issues and a house divided could not stand". I told him "I was always told not to marry a sinner, but she is more of a Christian then any person I have ever known. I was very confused. I shared this with her, and she was very hurt that my pastor would recommend this. She went to her grandmother, which was the cornerstone in this family when it came to their Christian life.

To our amazement her grandmother also said not to marry me, because we would have relationship issues over our beliefs. I was determined that after finding a Christian girl, that I would not let this stand between us. I found myself going to her church most of the time. I knew there was something with her belief, because of how different they all dressed and acted. We agreed we would not let this get between our love and the love would be stronger.

Making a Family on Earth and in Heaven

I took a job at a local retailer and decided that I would go to work in the coal mines to be able to marry and support her. This is another time in my life that I look back at amazement how God was leading me down the path he wanted me to go. When I finally decided to work in the coal mines, they were not hiring and for the first time in years you had to wait 6 months to a year to get a job. I was excelling at the retail store that I worked at, and they asked me to go into their management training program and I agreed. I received a pay increase, so I sat down with her and put everything on paper on how I could pay for us if she agreed to marry me. She trusted me way too much and said yes. We got married and as you could probably guess we were expecting not long after. I will never forget the night God brought my son into the world. We were on our normal Friday night routine at our local McDonalds when she told me that her water broke. The only problem was we were a little over one hour from the hospital. I rushed her to the little car we had, which had problems with the passenger door shutting in the past, but on this night the door would not shut. I slammed the door repeatedly trying to get the latch to connect to no luck as she got louder and louder. I then jumped in the driver's seat and for a 30-minute drive to my parents I kept my right hand on her door handle holding it together while I drove. It seemed like a lifetime. I drove this road twice daily for five days a week to work, but on this night, I cannot even remember how we made it from that restaurant to my parents. The louder she screamed the louder I prayed. I knew God was driving that car that night, or we would have never made it. When we got to the hospital, they took her back and I was so nervous. I can remember her doctor coming up to me and telling me everything would be fine and asking if I still wanted to be in the labor room with her and I said yes not knowing what I was going to be faced with. My wife was so scared, but when she saw me enter the room, I could see her relax a little and the doctor made us laugh when he said "See, I told you 8 months ago it would happen on 11/1, so why are you looking surprised"? I looked at my wife and said he did give us this date. Again, I felt the calm come over me like when I was 5 and I knew God was in control.

We soon found ourselves with a promotion at my work, a new city to live in, and another baby on the way. We already had a beautiful boy and now a blue-eyed little girl who captured my heart. The one thing that was missing was time to walk and talk to God. We had been so busy with moving to a new city and two small babies that we really did not attempt to attend church. One day my wife asked me to go to her family's church with her next weekend. I replied, "Why don't we go to my old church". It was at that time that we both realized that we were going to have some issues over this. We got into an argument and at that time we did not even know what the real differences the churches had. She asked me a very insulting question "Just how many gods do you serve". I studied her for a minute and said, "What do you mean". She answered, "There is only one God and his name is Jesus". I looked at her and said, "We know who Jesus is, so what are you trying to say". She replied, "You believe in the trinity which is three gods". I said, "Yes I believe in the trinity, but I do not serve three gods". She replied, "Yes you do"! I was so upset at her that night that I knew I said some things that I would regret later and boy did I have some apologizing to do.

I came back to her the next night and apologized to her and asked if we could read the Bible like we used to and talk about what we read. She accepted my apology and we tried to read the Bible together, but it was never the same after that. We now started separating ourselves from how we believed. We got into more arguments over the Bible then living as husband and wife. At one point I thought my pastor and her grandmother was right. We then got caught up in the talk that everyone believed the rapture was going to happen in the late 1980's. I read and study the Bible a lot, so I stood on the scripture that says no man will know the day or the hour, but it was still convincing enough to get me to put my stubborn ways aside and go with my wife to church. I knew she would not go to my church, so after months of not going to any church I knew I needed to go somewhere. During one of the services, I felt the Spirit came upon me in a way I have never felt before. I had always been in control of my emotions and my body, but on this night, I let God control me. I joined the service and there were people shouting, dancing, and running all around the church. I am not sure what all I did, but I joined in and praised God like I have never done before. One of the ministers came up to me and asked me if I have ever been baptized in the name of Jesus Christ like it was done in the book of Acts. I told him I had been baptized in the name of the Father, Son, and Holy Ghost. He asked me if I would like to be baptized in the name of Jesus Christ and told me that the Holy Ghost would come upon me in ways I haven't felt before. I said "Yes" and I was baptized that night in the name of Jesus Christ. When I came out of the water, I began praising him like I did earlier, and I felt like I did when I was 14. I felt like I could just fly away. Later that night I taught a bible lesson to one of my wife's aunts. I could not stop talking about God's word that I have been studying for years. My wife was so happy and proud of me that night.

The next day I started questioning everything again and I did not understand the Bible like I thought I did. My wife asked me about the trinity again and we ended up in the same argument as before. I told her I know there was something going on with her church, but

I could not see it in the Bible. We still could not read and study together as it would end up in an argument. However, I started attending regularly with her at her church now. We took the approach that we would not debate it anymore.

My Eyes Opening

A couple of years later we received another promotion, and I was asked to be the store manager in Norton, VA. This is the first time we have lived outside of West Virginia and Kentucky. We were too far from our hometown area to attend our old churches, and we found ourselves in the same debate about what church do we find in this new place. We hadn't gone to any churches because my wife only wanted to go to one like hers and we could not find one. I really was not looking very hard. It was easier not to attend church than to give in and go to the one she wanted. But of course, God will always intervene to get me back on the path that he wants me on.

On a Saturday afternoon I am at the service desk, and a lady comes in for a refund. I process the return and she asked, "Are you new to the store". I said "Yes, I just took this store over about 3 months ago". She replied, "Do you have a family". I said "Yes, I have a wife and two kids". She then asked, "Do you like it in this area". I said "Yes, but we do not get out much because the kids are very small". She replied, "I understand, but I guess you at least get out and go to church on Sunday's". I said, "We have not found a church yet, but I am sure we will in time". She then told me her name was Connie and handed me a card with her church information on it. I looked at the name of the church and sure enough it was the kind of church my wife attends. Immediately I looked down to see if this lady was wearing a dress. Of course she was not just wearing a dress, but it was long and down to her ankles. She was not wearing any makeup, and her hair was down past her waist. I was very polite to her and told her I would talk to my wife about it. I wanted to throw the card away as soon as she walked away. Instead, I placed it in my wallet, but I had no intention of showing my wife this card.

About 2 weeks later my son is playing on our porch and he sliced his finger on some of the metal underpinning I had recently put up. His finger was almost cut into and as we rushed him to the hospital,

I found myself praying to God to take care of him. It seems wrong to go months without really walking, talking, or spending anytime with God, but as soon as a tragedy hits, I go to him, and of course he is always there waiting on me. My son's finger required several stitches, but God took care of him. I do not even think he has a scare left from this which again makes me think that God wanted to get my attention and get me back on the path he wants me on. Later that night my wife was very emotional how she missed going to church and how she knows she is letting God down. I pulled the card out of my wallet and shared it with her, and I had not seen her smile like that in a very long time. The following Sunday we went to church and yes it was like the churches I attended with her in our old town. People were freely worshipping God throughout the service thru shouting, dancing, clapping, and yes at times running around the church. The lady who gave me the card and her husband very quickly bonded with us, and they had a son of their own. They soon became our friends, and we would go places after church with them and talk. It really felt good to have them as friends in a strange place where we did not know anyone. The main hang out after church for us was McDonalds which put in the kids play area and while the kids were busy playing, we had time to have quality conversations. I know my wife was happy for the first time since we took this transfer.

It only took a few weeks before we had one of our arguments about our beliefs again. I tried to get her to study in the book of Hebrews with me so I could show her how my beliefs made more sense. She would not listen to me and kept repeating a couple of verses about there is only one God and the devils know it and tremble. I could not get her to read several scriptures so I could get her to see the big picture. Finally, I decided what I would do. The next time we go with our friends after church to McDonalds I will accept his request to teach me a bible study. The following Sunday we all went out after church and I said "Donnie, you have been wanting to teach me a bible study, and I would love to learn more". Donnie replied with a huge smile "Oh, that would be great. When can we get together". I said, "What about this Tuesday at my house around 6 PM". He said "Great". I knew that if I could bring him to my house and convince him he is wrong then my wife would listen to me. Donnie was so excited to have the opportunity to share a bible study with me he started talking about it right then. I wanted to prepare my scriptures, so I told him I was very eager to listen to him, but let's wait until Tuesday.

I studied and prepared myself Monday evening, so I would be ready for our meeting. I highlighted scripture after scripture so I would not get nervous and forget the flow I wanted to go to show him how I believe. Donnie showed up on Tuesday evening with a huge smile as I invited him in. We sat down and I said "Donnie, before we get started, I would like the opportunity to share some things in the Bible with you first". He replied "Sure. That sounds great but let us pray first". We started to pray and I noticed this man had a lot of confidence and I could tell he was comfortable talking out loud with God. After we stopped praying, he allowed me to begin. I started reading the highlighted scriptures one after another and adding what I thought they meant. He kept smiling and listening to me. Wow! I was so excited because he listened and did not challenge anything I said. My wife would debate every scripture I would try and share with her to the point where it became an argument and I could not piece them together for her. But Donnie listened and made comments like really and I see that, which made me think I have really got my message across to him. Finally, after about an hour I asked him "So, what do you think". He looked at me and said, "You really put a lot of thought into this and you really made a very compelling argument on how you believe". He went on and said "Here is what I would like you to do. I want you to show me a scripture in the Bible where someone was baptized in the name of the Father, Son, and Holy Ghost and I will believe and follow everything you said". I looked at him with a doubting face and said "Really". He replied "Yes". I thought to myself that will not be hard after all that was the great commission from Jesus in Matthew chapter 28. I started looking up verse after verse and referring to the concordance. After about 15 minutes Donnie said "I tell you what. Take your time and call me tomorrow with the scripture". I agreed and he left.

I started reading scripture after scripture and chapter after chapter. I was studying the Bible in a way that I haven't for years. I read scriptures in Acts where people were baptized in the name of Jesus Christ, but I could not find one where they were baptized in the name of the Father, Son, and Holy Ghost. I looked at the clock, and it was now 2 AM and I was still looking. I became very humbled and I started to pray and ask God to show me. Around 4 AM I felt something come over

me and it was like a cool breeze and my eyes opened
and every scripture I read made more sense than in the
past and I was getting different interpretations out of
them. I began crying and praising God. I do not think
I slept at all that night, and I was so furious the next
day. I thought to myself. If I was taught wrong on this
concept, what else have I allowed myself to believe that
may not be correct? You know I never called Donnie
back the next day and we never discussed this again.
He did not even ask about this conversation, which
again confirmed to me that God was in control and
still leading me down a certain path.

The Miracle

I did find myself on new ground now and wanting to read the entire Bible over again to see if I missed something else. I started looking at things less with my intelligence and more with exactly what it is saying. I really allowed myself to take part in church services and I really enjoyed it. When you read the story of David he was dancing and obviously enjoying himself so much that he got his wife's attention which embarrassed her. I told myself there is nothing wrong with enjoying yourself in God's presence. I looked forward to going to church as much as an amusement park. It was very interactive and a four-hour church service would only feel like one hour. I can remember a tent revival that we went to. There must have been over 300 people crowded under that tent, and we were all in wooden folding chairs. The preacher started preaching on the crucifixion of Jesus Christ and his illustration was so detailed. All the sudden you could feel the Spirit move in waves through this congregation and you would have thought you were in the lower stand at your favorite football team who won the championship on a touchdown throw as time ended on the clock. There were people dancing, shouting, praising, clapping, falling out in the spirit, and running everywhere. I do not recall what I did, but I know I joined them. There must have been at least two hours to pass that I do not even remember. I was experiencing things I have never experienced before with my walk with God.

It was only a couple of months later that my company asked me to move to Charleston, WV to run a new store they were opening in Belle. It would bring us closer to our hometown, and it would pay more money, so I accepted. This time I did not waste any time helping us find a church and we were recommended to a church in North Charleston. This was a very large church, and the pastor was very highly thought of in the church organization. He was constantly on crusades overseas, and we were told of times where two to three thousand were saved in one day after some of his messages. We were very excited to attend his church, but we did not see him very often due to his travels. Soon after we got there, we found out we were now expecting our third child.

My wife had several complications with her back carrying the baby and it was a very difficult pregnancy. Nothing prepared us for what we would be faced with when she delivered though. Again, I find myself relying on God to come thru for me once again. The doctor came into the delivery room and let us know it was time. I was dressed in the outfit they gave me and the only thing showing was my eyes. I was standing next to my wife ready to help her deliver our second daughter and all sudden four other people walked in with special equipment. The doctor said "The baby will be coming out soon so do not worry about the other people. They are here only for precautions". I asked him, "What precautions". He said, "Do not worry and everything will be fine". He then continued "The baby lost her heartbeat at different times based on the monitors and they are only here if we need them, but everything will be fine". I know my wife started to panic and I reassured her what the doctor said and that everything was going to be okay. I started praying as I saw our beautiful daughter come out. She did not cry at first and immediately the doctor cut the umbilical cord and gave her to one of the specialists with the equipment. And about the time I looked up to God, I heard our baby finally burst out crying. I started crying and hugging my wife, trying to reassure it was all going to work out. A few minutes later they let us hold her but said they need to keep her in the incubator for a little while. Later we find out that she has two holes in her heart. One was very small and they thought it would close with no problems, but the other was the size of a dime and they were concerned about it.

On our first appointment back with the pediatrician when she was 6 weeks old, they took ex-rays of her heart and showed it to us. They said the larger hole was not closing and it may require surgery. They told us it was important not to let her get sick and to be very careful with her. They told us they could not really do anything until she was at least 1 year old. My wife looked at me and said, "We need to call the pastor and have him pray to heal her heart". I replied, "I am sure they are already praying for her, but we should call them". My wife then said, "No. I mean to take her up for a healing prayer to make her whole". I looked at her and agreed. I have seen a lot of things in her church, but I will admit I was a little doubtful about this one. I know God can heal who he pleases, but to take our baby to a minister to pray over her heart to be made whole again was asking for a lot. My wife called the church and told them what was going on and they told her the pastor would be back in town that week and they would have him call her back. In a couple of days, the pastor called my wife and told her to make sure we were in church on Sunday and he would call us up when he was ready for the healing prayer. During the church service you could feel the Spirit moving and then the pastor stood up and asked us to bring our baby to the front and he met us in front of the alter. He anointed himself first and then the baby and he looked at us. He said, "Do you have faith that God will heal your baby". My wife said with tears flowing down her eyes "Yes". I also said yes and I thought back when my dad was dying how God listened to me as a child and I said, "Please Lord". The pastor began praying and again I felt a cool breeze come over us and my wife started praising and shouting and fell out in the Spirit. I continued holding our baby and I am not sure exactly what the pastor was saying, but I felt the authority of God right there. I really cannot describe it, but it was different.

The following Friday we had another appointment and when they hooked the machines to our baby the doctor whispered, "It's a miracle". My wife looked at him and said, "What did you say". The doctor replied "I was thinking out loud. I need more reports and we will discuss this on Monday". He finished the test he was running and gave us an appointment time to meet him in his office on Monday. My wife was so excited and started calling family and the church. There was such a peaceful spirit at church on Sunday, but the pastor was out of town again. Everyone at the church came up to us giving us their support and told us they would continue to pray for a good report. I do not think my wife slept Sunday night. She was so excited to get back to the doctor's office. We arrived at least 1 hour prior to our appointment and of course they called us back 30 minutes after the appointment time. We sat there very patiently in the doctor's office waiting for him to come in. He finally showed up and he knew we were very anxious to hear what he had to say. He smiled at us and said, "I sent the reports off to get a second opinion and just got them back". He went on to say, "We have confirmed that the large hole is no longer there and the small hole is still there, but that is not the one we were worried about". My wife burst out in tears and all I could say in front of the doctor was "Thank you Lord". The doctor then said it was truly a miracle. He told us that he would not need to see our baby again for 12 months and set us up an appointment. At the age of 2 years old our daughter was confirmed not to have any heart murmurs of any kind. It was in fact a true miracle!

UNDERSTANDING THE END TIMES

A few years passed and I decided to take an opportunity with a different company and we moved to Omaha, NE. Yes, I said Omaha, NE. That was a big move for a country boy and his family, but I look back and again I can now see the path that God had me on. We were struggling financially trying to support a family of five on my current income and my wife for the first time decided to help by taking a part time job that would work around my schedule. It put more space between us, and we did not have a lot of time to spend together. When I presented this opportunity to her, she was very skeptical, but she did see the opportunity to improve our financial status. Again, my wife trusted me way too much and I accepted the offer to go. I remember when we told my parents we were moving to Nebraska, my mom asked if it was close to Ohio. It was hard to tell them that we would be over a 20-hour drive away. They tried to get us to change our minds, but God made certain that would not happen. I told my current employer the idea that I was prepared to do and would give him at least a 30-day notice. At one time I thought about changing my mind, but then the owner of the company I worked for let me know he was promoting his son to my job, and he did not have a spot for me. I made sure I did not leave them on bad terms, but I knew that the move to Nebraska was the only option now.

We lived in Nebraska for almost 6 years and my kids bonded more there with all their neighborhood friends than any other place we had been. We found a church there that really made us feel at home. I had an opportunity to take a promotion with my new company and became a district manager over their stores in Nebraska and Iowa. It kept me on the road a lot, which was not the best for my family. I did however use all the time driving as an opportunity to listen to a lot of bible tapes. I guess I was at the point that I saw a lot of the beliefs now from my wife's church. I would still read and study to make sure I understood them, so I could support what I was seeing and still support my take on things that I saw a little differently. During one of the church services a new pastor came who was starting a new ministry and wanted some of our church families to come and visit his new missionary church as much as possible. He started a lesson on the early church and taught it from the book of Acts one chapter at a time. It was so clear and really helped me continue to connect my beliefs with their beliefs and I made certain I went to every lesson. Once he finished that lesson, he started a lesson on understanding the end times put together by a minister named Irvin Baxter. During the first class he taught us some scriptures that would help us understand how nations are mentioned in the Bible and how to understand the 4 horsemen. One night he described John the revelator so we could understand more what he wrote about. The minister told us John is describing things that he is being shown from the future but does not know what they are. All John can do is use an illustration from his time to try and describe what he is seeing. The minister had us read some scriptures in Revelations.

zzzzz

And the shapes of the locusts were like unto horses prepared unto battle: and their heads were as it were crowns like gold, and their faces were as the faces of men. And they had hair as the hair of women, and their teeth were as the teeth of lions. And they had breastplates, as it were breastplates of iron; and the sound of their wings was as the sound of chariots of many horses running to battle. And they had tails like unto scorpions, and there were stings in their tails: and their power was to hurt men five months.

Revelations 9:7-10 (KJV)

zzzzz-end

The minister went on to ask us what we thought John was describing. Then the minister asked us if we thought it could be a helicopter. He then asked us to close our eyes and imagine we had never seen a helicopter before and then he started to break it down. He pointed out that John said it had a face like unto a man and if you looked straight into a helicopter, you would see a man's face with a helmet on. He asked us to think about what the propellers would look like in mid air and could it look like hair spinning. He said think about the breast plate of iron and the front of the helicopter and the noise a helicopter made might be compared to the sound of horses running to battle. I was stunned to see that a man of God almost 2000 years ago described a helicopter and obviously was looking into the future. Now I really can read Revelations with a better understanding of what John is trying to tell us.

One day after that I started listening to one of my bible tapes and I had it on Revelations and as it was being read I visualized what John was saying, and it shocked me. I was at a red light, so I picked up my co-pilot which is my Bible and opened it to the scripture to see if it was narrated word for word. I got so lost in what I could now visualize that I forgot I was stopped and hit the gas and rear ended the car in front of me. It was an eye-opening event and a lesson to be learned at the same time. Keep your eyes on the road and pay attention when you are behind the wheel.

Not long after that my company asked us to move to Dallas, TX and take over a more challenging district. The money was more and I would be home every night. We accepted the transfer and I lived up to the promises I gave my kids. They did not want to leave their friends in Nebraska, so they wanted a house with an upstairs and a swimming pool. I found the perfect house on my first trip house hunting and again I can see where God helped my family accept the new area that we were moving too. The farthest store I would be overseeing was only 50 miles away, which also made it easier on a balance of work and family life. We found another quality church in Euless, TX, but more importantly we were now living in an area where Irvin Baxter had his own radio segment and would come to this area for summits quite often. I would listen to his broadcast as much as possible and would always go to his summits. I learned things under his ministry like what happens at the rapture and more about the 1000-year millennium. I know there is a big debate over pre-tribulation or post tribulation. His teachings were very detailed in the scriptures and helped me understand this better. I have always heard how Jesus will rule 1000 years on Earth, but you really do not think about it. Irvin shows where it describes it in the scriptures and it helped me understand it better and opened my eyes to a lot of things and what to watch for related to signs of the final days. I have heard this from a lot of religious leaders that we should not get wrapped up in post or pre-tribulation, but just "Be ready". We are living in the end time now and I think we all know it.

CAN GOD REALLY TALK TO YOU

It seemed that life was good, but then my dad had an unexpected heart attack. I did not realize how far from our families we were until this happened. It took me 19 hours to drive straight and that was only stopping for quick naps in the car and gas. My dad had an enlarged heart and the doctors said he will never be 100% again with a life expectancy of less than 10 years. When an opportunity came up to move to the East coast I talked to my family and reluctantly they came. I would ask God what he wanted from me. I would hear stories how people would say God talked to them, but I did not think that could happen. Yes, he could talk to us in our dreams, or he would put thoughts in our minds, but not an actual voice. Regardless I would ask him to talk to me and tell me what he wants from me.

We have moved to so many different places and now we are moving to northern Virginia. I know this was very hard on my kids. My two oldest kids are now in high school, and this move would be very difficult for them. They agreed to come because they knew it would get us closer to our families and this is one move; they did it to please me. Now I find myself spending more time at work due to the traffic and the distance some of the stores were from our house. I ask God why we are moving around so much and why are we in this place. I never got a response.

We found a small church with about six families in it, and it made us feel at home again. I have never participated in a church since I was a teenager, but they needed as much help as possible. The past church was so large that you could get lost in the numbers. I expressed my desire to the pastor that I would like to help as much as possible. He explained his platform ministry rules and let me know if I did not qualify for any of those types of services, then there were plenty of other things I could do around the church. We moved to a very expensive place to live and with three teenagers, money was very tight. We also had some bills left over from the move which added to the financial obligations where we live now. Due to that I could not pay my full 10% tithing which was one of the platform ministry rules, but I would give what I could. I really respected and honored the pastor for staying true to his platform commitments and I would help on as many workdays around the church as I could. During the summer I would maintain the lawn most of the time and that was a big task with all the land that was with the church. I really got close with the pastor and his family by staying involved in helping them around the church.

It was just over a year since we had moved here, and my wife's father passed away very unexpectedly. It was comforting knowing we were closer to them, and we could spend more time with the family. My dad's heart also weakened, and the doctors were having a difficult time finding medicine that would work with his heart and blood to keep it stable. We had a visiting preacher come to our church, and he had the gift of healing. After his message he began calling people out in the congregation and telling them what issues they were having in their bodies and asking them to come forward for prayer. After witnessing my daughter being healed I knew this gift is out there and God is using it. I was standing up front with my wife and two daughters, when a lady who had an issue with her hand came forward. It was bruised and blue and she told him the doctors wanted to set her up for surgery later that week. I was praying with my family and was standing next to them. I saw the preacher put his hand on her hand and began to pray. I saw her hand change colors right in front of me and even her arm returned to the natural skin color. I asked my daughter if she saw that and she said yes.

I went back to my seat, and my youngest daughter saw me and came over to me. She asked "Dad, why don't you ask him to prey for your dad". I looked around and I saw the preacher sitting in a corner. You could tell he was exhausted. I went over to him and said, "I hate to bother you, but I have a need". He looked into my eyes and said, "It is for someone very close to you, but they live far away, right". I said "Yes, it is my dad". He then said, "Your dad struggles with heart problems right". And again, I said "Yes" with tears coming down my face. He then said, "Let's prey". We began to prey and then I noticed the preacher stopped. I looked up at him, and he was looking at me. The preacher said "Son, your dad will not be healed, but we can pray for more time". He asked me if I had a handkerchief and I said no. He pulled one out and told me it was clean and he had not used it. He prayed over the handkerchief, and he told me to give this to my dad, and it will help. I called my mom later that night and asked how he was doing. She told me not well and they were going to try another medicine on him. The following Saturday I took the handkerchief down to them and I gave it to my mom. I told her what I had experienced, and she told me she would place it inside the pillowcase of the pillow he sleeps with. The next week when he went to the doctor, they said his blood was now in line and they would not have to try a different medicine.

A few months later I was driving to work, and I had a Christian CD playing and I was praising God in my car. I knew I heard something, so I thought it was my phone, and I turned the music down. It was not my phone, so I turned the music back up. All a sudden I heard a voice like it was someone sitting in the passenger seat. I turned the music back down, but now it was quiet. I continued to drive leaving the music off and as plain as having a conversation with another person I heard a voice say "Roger, you will lose someone close to you this year". I started looking around and I was in shock. I then said, "If that was you God, please let me know for sure so I do not convince myself I am hearing things". A few seconds later I heard it again and it said you will lose someone close to you. I began crying and asking him who and why. I never heard anything else. I thought it was my dad, and I shared this with my youngest daughter. She said to spend as much time with him as possible. About 3 months later we were visiting our family and dad was looking better. I asked mom if the prayer cloth was still in his pillow and she said yes and smiled at me. On our last day before going back we were spending time with my wife's mom, and she told my wife that she had a lump in her chest and she was going to have it checked out. Later that week she was diagnosed with stage 4 cancer. I was furious with God for telling me what he did. I did not know what to do but pray for her. I needed to be supportive to my wife and family that she is going to be okay. All along I am walking around with what God told me. What should I do I thought.

My mother-in-law passed away merely 5 months after being diagnosed. This was a woman who has never been sick and never goes to a doctor. She passed away within the same year as when I heard that voice.

In prayer I would cry and ask why he would do that to me. Was I supposed to do something with it to help someone. If that was the case I failed, because I did not tell anyone but my daughter. During prayer I did not hear a voice, but it came over me that God was letting me know he does talk to people.

God Gives Life and He Takes It

We found out my oldest daughter was pregnant. It was going to be our first grandbaby. My daughter and her husband were as excited about it as we were. They were struggling to make it in Northern Virginia, so they came back to our hometown where we grew up and my son in law took a job in the coalmines. For a young man it was no pleasure job because they would work him 6 days a week and long hours each day. My daughter was bored and wanted to join us on our vacation to the beach. We were more than excited to get to spend time with her, so I took off with my wife and two daughters. It will be a vacation that we will never forget. My daughters were so excited to go and watch a show at Medieval Times. It was dinner and a show, and we had never experienced anything like that before. I will never forget the look on my wife's face when they tossed that big turkey leg on the metal plate in front of her. She said, "That is disgusting and we should not eat it". Then we looked over to my oldest daughter, and she had her turkey leg up to her mouth and was tearing the meat off with her teeth and said "Yum". My wife said, "You are sick" and we all laughed at her while we ate our turkey legs. The show did not end until after 9 PM and we left there around 10. My daughter started complaining about stomach cramps while we were driving back to the room. It got so bad we decided to pull into a hospital to get her checked, but the wait could be 6 to 7 hours before they would be able to take her back to a room. We decided to go on to the motel room and see if she started feeling better. She was about 4 months pregnant, and the cramps only got stronger as the night went on. We made the decision about 5 AM to pack up and start driving back to Virginia where her doctor was. It was about a 7-hour drive, but after about 3 hours she said she had to go to the bathroom. We pulled off and she had a miscarriage at the gas station and we called the ambulance. I thought I was losing my daughter and grandbaby at that time. I held her until the ambulance showed up. She was devastated! I will never forget when I walked in her room and she said, "Why Daddy". I told her to trust God, and it will be okay.

It was less than one year, and she got pregnant again and this time she had a beautiful baby girl. My wife and I got so attached to her and she was our joy. She was 1 year old when she came down with a fever due to an ear infection. Her fever was running over 104% and eventually my daughter took her to the hospital since we could not get it down. My daughter called me crying and said the baby had gone into a comma, and the doctors did not know what to do. They said she was having seizures due to the high temperatures, and they could not get it down. I jumped in my truck, and I was praying all the way to the hospital. For the second time I heard the same voice as I heard before. It said very clearly that she would be okay. I asked for confirmation, but this time I did not hear it again. I got to the ER, and her little body was lifeless. The machines were breathing for her. I started praying there as well, but nothing was happening. My daughter was very upset, and I hugged her and I told her God said she would be okay. Trust and believe what God said. We both started crying more. After about 30 minutes they were still not having any luck, and the decision was made to fly her to a hospital in DC. I again asked God, "Please let her be okay. We cannot bare this again". The doctor gave her something else and said this needs to work to get her temperature down so they can move her. In about 10 minutes her fever broke, and they proceeded to fly her to DC. I had heard his voice for the second time, and I knew she was going to get better.

The Assignment

I t still seems like we have been on a journey as a family. I still ask God why I have experienced so many different places and things along the way. We went back to visit family in Kentucky again and we are now planning on moving back to where we grew up. We left about 14 years ago, and we feel it's time to think about going back. The decision to go back is very difficult for my wife since she has lost both of her parents over the previous 2 years. She is also struggling with leaving our grand baby in Northern Virginia. It was a quiet ride back home after the visit. My wife had a lot on her mind, and I was trying to decide what was the right move in God's eyes. I was going over scriptures in my head, when all a sudden I heard the voice again and it said, "Read John chapter 3". I looked around and my wife had her eyes closed. I then started trying to remember the scriptures in this chapter. I know this is the chapter where Jesus talks to Nicodemus and answers the question, which is how to get to Heaven.

Later that night when we got home, I could not wait to go and read the chapter. I read it and I did not see anything different than I have in the past. The next morning, I was going to work so I put it on the audio and listened to it repeatedly. This time something stood out. Jesus is telling him how to get to Heaven and talks about being born again. Nicodemus could not understand what he was saying. Then Jesus changed from what he was saying and is now telling him what to do to have everlasting life. I noticed these are two completely different responses. Then I asked myself "Why". I noticed the response that Jesus gave him in John 3:12 (KJV) "If I have told you earthly things, and ye believe not, how shall ye believe, if I tell you of heavenly things". So how could Nicodemus understand a heavenly response when he could not even understand an earthly response. Then Jesus went on to say in John 3:13 (KJV) "And no man hath ascended up to heaven, but he that came down from heaven, even the Son of man which is in heaven". Then I noticed Jesus is saying that no man has ascended to heaven. That made me think back on the story of Elijah when he was carried away in a chariot of fire. Where did he go if no man has ever ascended to heaven? And then I finally saw what God was trying to show me. The answer came in John 3:15 (KJV) "That whosoever believeth in him should not perish but have eternal life". Jesus went from telling Nicodemus how to get to heaven to how to have eternal life. And then I literally shouted out "There was two promises in this encounter with Nicodemus"!

Hopefully I have not lost any of my readers, but I have simply got your attention. I am not telling you a story to bring more controversy to the whole issue revolving around all the religious beliefs, but it answered a question that has been haunting me since God opened my eyes the night, I saw baptism in a different light. I have been on this journey which has mentally torn me apart. I have struggled with difference of opinions with my wife, being confused on why it seemed so few people actually saw the things I have been experiencing, and the biggest weight of all was if this is correct where does that leave so many members of my family and friends who does not see and believe the way my wife's church does. God showed me there were two promises and I was so excited to share this with my wife and people I know. I wanted to make sure that I truly had a clear understanding of this first, so I surfed the web looking for any possible literature out there related to what I was shown, but I could not find any. I shared this with my wife and son-in-law, and both listened but were very skeptical. I then feared that if I presented this to my pastor it would leave me with no true church to be a part of. It seemed like the more questions around this area I asked, the more opposition I had. The most frequent comment I received would be that I need to be careful. God has opened your eyes to see the truth, and you are trying to go backwards. I then went back to God and asked him why me and what do I do with this. Months went by and I had no response, but the more I would read the scriptures the more that other parts would open my eyes to a different understanding.

Finally, I got my answer. I have had an opportunity to live on both sides of the road related to the two church organizations. Most members of my wife's church organization were born into it and raised into this understanding. I was raised under a Baptist understanding of the bible and was very engaged in learning as much as I could about God and then married into the Apostolic understanding. I argued the ideals of this belief, but God was very firm in keeping my family together even when most of the fights I experienced with my wife was due to the differences in our beliefs. It took almost 8 years before I came to the reality that the way they baptized was supported in the book of Acts and by Peter who Jesus said in Matthew:

zzzzz

"And I say also unto thee, that thou art Peter, and upon this rock I will build my church; and the gates of hell shall not prevail against it. And I will give unto thee the keys of the kingdom of heaven: and whatsoever thou shalt bind on earth shall be bound in heaven: and whatsoever thou shalt loose on earth shall be loosed in heaven".

Matthew 16:18 -19 (KJV)

zzzzz-end

If Peter baptized in the name of Jesus Christ, then I knew I could not debate that. Then when I had the opportunity to go through the end-time studies through the teaching of Irvin Baxter I came to a better understanding of what happens during and after the great tribulation. I also had the opportunity to not only be a part of seeing miracles performed in the church, but having my own daughter healed. I see now that God wants me to send a message out so that some of the divisions between so many churches would come down. We all know that the more Satan can keep Christians debating Christians, the more he keeps us from being more focused on bringing more souls to salvation. We are all part of one church, and we need to be united and not divided.

And then God spoke to me again and asked me to write a book. I have not read more than two other books in my life other than the Bible. I told God that I do not know how to write a book and again I have had no answer back from him. I fought this idea for months and really tried to run from it. I took the new job and moved to Kentucky. I tried to put all my focus into this new job trying to hide from what God has asked me to do. I have become more distanced from my previous friends, and I have noticed more controversy between beliefs with my wife over the past few months. I finally said yes and started writing my story and I am trusting God to give me the words to describe the two promises he has shown me.

Understanding The Two Promises

L et's go back to John chapter 3 for a few minutes. Nicodemus asked how to get to heaven. What does Jesus mean in verse 3 when he says you must be born again? He tells Nicodemus in verse 5 you must be born of the water and the spirit to be able to enter the kingdom of God. This experience tied with the rapture gives us a body that can enter the kingdom of Heaven. We will talk more about this later, but I want you to notice that he changed his words when he knew Nicodemus was not understanding what he was saying. He now goes into a very famous verse in John chapter 3 and verse 16 when he describes the love of God and how believing on him would give you ever lasting life. I am sure it is where we all read this and think it means the same. If you get into heaven then we know we will have everlasting life, right?

This takes me to what I learned in the end time teachings now. I know we have all read about some of the events that will happen at the end time. We know that there will be a new heaven and a new earth. We also read about the 1000-year millennium, and we know that it is still coming, but I think we see that as part of the afterlife. I know we read about the Great White throne judgment, where we hope to hear that our name is in the book of life. I know we read about rapture and there is always a lot of controversy about post or pre-tribulation. If we all read about all these events, why do we not question the timeline of each of them more?

I would like to ask you three questions:

1) What is the promise given in the rapture?

*In Corinthians we find that we will be changed before the last trumpet, which also gives us a time in history when it will happen which we have read in Revelations that the last trumpet happens at the end of the great tribulation. This could indicate its during the 6th trumpet.

zzzzz

"In a moment, in the twinkling of an eye, at the last trump: for the trumpet shall sound, and the dead shall be raised incorruptible, and we shall be changed."

I Corinthians 15:52 (KJV)

zzzzz-end

*In the 19th chapter of Revelations, we find that the bride has been called to the marriage supper. We must understand that they were called and notice they were given fine linen, clean, and white.

zzzzz

"Let us be glad and rejoice and give honor to him: for the marriage of the Lamb comes, and his wife hath made herself ready. And to her it was granted that she should be arrayed in fine linen, clean and white: for the fine linen is the righteousness of saints. And he saith unto me, Write Blessed are they which are called unto the marriage supper of the Lamb. And he saith unto me, these are the true sayings of God."

Revelations 19:7-9 (KJV)

zzzzz-end

*Also, in the 19th chapter of Revelations we find that the armies that followed Jesus to Armageddon was clothed in fine linen, clean and white.

zzzzz

"And the armies which were in heaven followed him upon white horses, clothed in fine linen, white and clean"

Revelations 19:14 (KJV)

zzzzz-end

*In the 20th chapter of Revelations, we find that those who are part of the first resurrection will reign with Christ for 1000 years and will not have any part of the second death.

zzzzz

"Blessed and holy is he that hath part in the first resurrection: on such the second death hath no power, but they shall be priests of God and of Christ and shall reign with him a thousand years. And when the thousand years are expired, Satan shall be loosed out of his prison and shall go out to deceive the nations which are in the four quarters of the earth, Gog and Magog, to gather them together to battle: the number of whom is as the sand of the sea."

Revelations 20:6-8 (KJV)

zzzzz-end

2) Who will be here during the 1000-year millennium?

*In the 20th chapter of Revelations, it tells us that those who were beheaded for his name, those that had not worshipped the beast, and those who did not receive the mark of the beast would live with him for 1000 years.

zzzzz

"And I saw thrones, and they sat upon them, and judgment was given unto them: and I saw the souls of them that were beheaded for the witness of Jesus, and for the word of God, and which had not worshipped the beast, neither his image, neither had received his mark upon their foreheads, or in their hands; and they lived and reigned with Christ a thousand years".

zzzzz-end

*Also, in the 20th chapter of Revelations it tells us the rest of the dead would not live again until after 1000 years.

zzzzz

"But the rest of the dead lived not again until the thousand years were finished. This is the first resurrection".

Revelations 20:5 (KJV)

zzzzz-end

*Also, in the 20th chapter of Revelations it tells us Satan would be bound for 1000 years and would not be able to deceive the nations anymore, which implies they are nations still on earth.

zzzzz

"And he laid hold on the dragon, that old serpent, which is the Devil, and Satan, and bound him a thousand years, And cast him into the bottomless pit, and shut him up, and set a seal upon him, that he should deceive the nations no more, till the thousand years should be fulfilled: and after that he must be loosed a little season."

Revelations 20:2-3 (KJV)

zzzzz-end

3) What is the promise given to those at the Great White throne judgment?

*In the 20th chapter of Revelations, it tells us the dead stood before God and were judged out of the book of life according to their works (the reward of having your name in the book of life, would be life).

zzzzz

"And I saw a great white throne, and him that sat on it, from whose face the earth and the heaven fled away: and there was found no place for them. And I saw the dead, small and great, stand before God; and the books were opened: and another book was opened, which is the book of life: and the dead were judged out of those things which were written in the books, accordingly to their works".

Revelations 20:11-12 (KJV)

zzzzz-end

*It goes on to tell us that death and hell were cast in the lake of fire as well as all those that did not have their name written in the book of life.

zzzzz

"And the sea gave up the dead which were in it; and death and hell delivered up the dead which were in them: and they were judged every man according to their works. And death and hell were cast into the lake of fire. This is the second death. And whosoever was not found in the book of life was cast into the lake of fire".

Revelations 20:13-15 (KJV)

zzzzz-end

*Daniel spoke of a time when all nations will be delivered to see if they are written in the book and even those that sleep in the dust of the earth shall be woken. He said some will wake up to everlasting life and some to shame and everlasting contempt.

zzzzz

"And at that time shall Michael stand up, the great prince which stand for the children of thy people: and there shall be a time of trouble, such as never was since there was a nation even to that same time: and at that time thy people shall be delivered, every one that shall be found written in the book. And many of them that sleep in the dust of the earth shall awake, some to everlasting life, and some to shame and everlasting contempt".

Daniel 12:1-2 (KJV)

zzzzz-end

I would also like you to think back in the parable of the talents and how Jesus compares that to the judgment of all nations in Matthew Chapter 25. He said he will divide them as sheep on his right hand and goats on his left hand. He said to the sheep on his right hand come and inherit the kingdom prepared for them. He said the goats on his left hand depart from me, because I never knew you and they will claim to have known him, but are cast out into everlasting punishment. I want you to realize that there are different timelines for events that will happen during the end time. That is why these 3 questions are so important that you search out your own answer to them, but please make sure you are satisfied with the answer you come up with. I would not have anyone to feel like I did that night when I realized that some of my beliefs were not based on the scriptures, but more on tradition. Please review and challenge yourself again with these 3 questions:

1) What is the promise given in the rapture?

2) Who will be here during the 1000-year millennium?

3) What is the promise given to this at the great white throne judgment?

The reason I want to challenge you on these three questions is because it goes back to the two promises spoken by Jesus in John chapter 3. When Jesus is telling Nicodemus about being born again, he is describing what it will take to be part of the rapture, which is the bride and is the first promise. Based on the first question I asked you I hope you understand that the bride is called up before the last trumpet to be with Christ for evermore. They are clothed in fine linen, clean and white and in Revelations chapter 8 verses 13-17 you will read that this group is described again, and it tells us that they are before the throne and will dwell alone side of Jesus forever. Notice they are called and during the second resurrection the people are delivered. When Nicodemus could not comprehend what Jesus was describing to him, Jesus then described the second promise which is believe upon his name and you should not perish but have ever lasting life. In verse 21 of John chapter 3 it tells us that those that doeth truth and come into the light that your deeds will become manifest and wrought with God. I do not mean to put thoughts in your head, but in other words you are in the book of life. It is important to understand the scriptures and be aware that the second promise is riskier than the first promise. Jesus said to those that were part of the rapture (The first promise) that they are blessed because they will not be part of the second death which is the great white throne judgment. They are permanently with God forever. Those that are part of the second promise will be judged to see if they are found in the book of life.

If anything at this point, I hope I have at least given you a headache because you are thinking about some of these things. I really do think that if you study this out you would agree that those in the rapture will not appear in judgment during the great white throne and it is obvious that there are two events. One is the rapture which is in the timeline of the great tribulation and the other is the great white throne judgment which is in the timeline of after the 1000-year millennium. You can read in Revelations chapter 20 where Satan is bound and then released after 1000 years. It is amazing that he can deceive the nations again after they have spent 1000 years in peace under the rule of Jesus and the saints that was part of the rapture, but he does. I think you would agree that if all those that lived in the 1000-year millennium were part of the rapture, there would be no way Satan could turn them against their Lord and savior. Then you can read how the nations in the 4 quarters of the earth who are deceived by Satan go up to make war with Jesus in the battle of Gog and Magog. This is when Jesus cast Satan in the lake of fire and devours the armies with fire. This is followed by the great white throne judgment.

Heading in Two Separate Paths

I can say without question that the decision to move to Kentucky is one of the bravest decisions I have ever made. I have now been working in Kentucky while my wife stays in the house we are renting in Virginia. I feel inside that she has no desire to join me in Kentucky and I fully understand why. The loss of her parents and leaving our grandchildren is too much for her to bear. Our pastor tried to talk me out of the decision and I feared the worse. He told me he saw a vision that I would be divorced from my wife in less than a year. He said after the vision he looked up the process of getting a divorce in Virginia and Kentucky and found out that you can have a legal divorce in Kentucky in about 90 days verses a longer waiting period in Virginia. That brought him to the conclusion that making the move would lead to a divorce. I begin to pray more to God and ask him what I should do. I have already left my job in Virginia and started the new job in Kentucky. It took weeks before I heard anything and during pray one day I heard something say, "Be Still". I did not know what that meant and I remembered the scripture where it said be still and wait upon the Lord. It was hard, but I kept still and worked hard at my new job to stay focused.

It had been over a year since I moved to Kentucky. I have still been struggling with writing this book and I work on it a little every few months. I still fight getting myself to write about what God wants me to say, so I ask him to help me put this into words. I have started attending the Baptist church that I grew up in when I was younger. I struggled with the message from the Apostolic churches I was hearing. I fully understand how they believe since God opened my eyes to their teachings as well as the two promises. It seems that ever since I saw the two promises it offends me when I hear them talk about other churches' beliefs in the pulpit and say they are going to hell if they continue their belief. I am struggling with this because Jesus said the most important things for us going forward is Hope, Faith. And Charity (love) and the greatest of these three is Charity. I did not feel comfortable anymore with this kind of message, because I did not feel the love for our fellow brothers and sisters. We are part of one church and God said you could not follow two masters' unless you hate one and love the other. So, no matter what religious following you have if it leads you thru the repentance of Jesus Christ and taking on his blood we are all serving one master and that is God. If we are all serving God, we should not fight amongst ourselves, but we need to be joined in the fight against Satan.

Finally, it was not just being "Still" that God wanted me to do. He opened my eyes to something even more important than the two promises. We need to put down the fences between religious beliefs and come together if we are going to participate in the greatest revival that this world has ever had. I started attending the Baptist church and the love and warmth they showed me was over whelming. It was like the prodigal son coming home. I have been attending there for several months now, and I have been very withdrawn. I sit in my seat, and I do not participate very much, but it helps me stay focused on what God is leading me to do. The one thing that I have noticed is their passion for the lost, who has never confessed their sins for the first time and took on the baptism. Every service they will preach to the lost more than to the saints and they have a passionate alter call asking for the lost to come. I have not seen this for years while I have been attending the Apostolic churches. It seems like they spend more time trying to convert a Christian from to their faith rather than seeking the actual lost sinners. I understand the importance of that because of what God showed me in the two promises. More blessed is he that is part of the first resurrection because he will not have to take part in the great white throne judgment and would rule with Christ for 1000 years. Versus living in the 1000 years or being resurrected to the great white throne judgment and hope that you have lived good enough to keep your name written in the Lambs book of life.

I truly have fallen in love with the desire to save the lost, because that was the great commission that Jesus gave us. Now do not take me wrong and believe I am saying that the Apostolic churches I attended did not seek to save the lost because they did. I am not saying that, but to a member who sits on the bench I am the hearer of the messages coming from the pulpit and most of the messages were to the saints to improve, or to convert. I also cannot tell you the last time one of those churches simply had an alter call and only asked the lost to come forward. On most occasions they would immediately ask all who would like to come and pray come forward and usually about 80% of the congregation would immediately come forward. Maybe I am a little old fashion, but when the pressure is on a sinner to step out on faith and walk down that aisle it is a true repentance. I can remember how hard it was to take that first step at 14 years of age and how heavy my feet felt like. But once I took the first step and my body moved forward the weights came off and it seemed like I floated to the front. Just in the last four weeks there has been at least three souls that came to repentance in the Baptist church that I am attending, and I watched as one young man who come to repentance a few months earlier has went from living in sin to now singing in the choir. All those that knew him would say he lived a rough life, and I would guess he had a lot of addictions to this world, but I get blessed every time I see him testify and start crying or when he is singing in the choir. Some people do not understand why I would attend the Baptist church and claims it is because I have family there. The fact is we have family in every church, because we are supposed to be one bride waiting for our groom. I know my wife believes if you do not believe in the way she does then you are going to hell and I still cannot get through to her. I will continue to trust in God that he will take care of things.

The Power of Unity

I hope one day that my wife and I can be united in the way we see our Christian lives. This is also the hope that I see in the world as well. I listened to my daughter tell me a story of a couple in our family that it appears their paths will end in divorce. They are a young couple, and I do not speak of this as if I know their lives, but they were both Christians of basically the same faith. They both believed in the Apostolic way, but on the husband's side they were very strict as how a Christian should live. A women should not cut her hair, or wear anything but dresses, or never wear make-up, and I am sure there were some other works that would be expected to live by to show their faith to God. However, the wife came from the same beliefs, but she did not feel it was wrong to cut your hair if it was still long or wear some foundation if it did not look like Jezebel, or wear something other than dresses as long as it was not in God's house or not indecent. Some of these issues as well as I am sure some other things lead them to an early departure from their marriage. It makes me think back when I planned to marry my wife and one of the ministers from my church told me not to marry her because of her beliefs and her grandmother telling her not to marry a Baptist person, because we would have problems and would not be equally yoked together. I write about this so we can all open our eyes and try and see thru God's eyes. When Jesus said we should not be unequally yoked together he was referring to one that is covered by his blood and one that is a sinner and loves this world. And even in that scenario he said to tolerate the unbeliever if they chose to stay with the believer because it could sanctify the unbeliever and they may come to repentance. Why would we allow these kinds of divisions to be among two believers.

Again, I go back to my frustration in religion, and I pray that we will see thru this entrapment that Satan has put out there for us. So, if you can truly see the power we would have if we united and put our differences aside it would in fact make Satan tremble.

The walls between religious beliefs are not thick walls, but we make them thick by feeding into it. If you can open your eyes and see that yes, we will always have different interpretations of the Bible, because that is the way God made us. Not to mention we are born into that because when Adam took of the fruit he wanted to be like God and that is the minds that we have today. That is why we struggle with so many different beliefs and in God's eyes I would believe he understands it. If you recall when Jesus was walking with his disciples and they heard a man preaching in a different way than they were they asked Jesus if they should go and rebuke him. What did Jesus say? He said who is not against us is for us. What did he mean by that? I know we will of course all have different interpretations, but if that man was preaching God, then he was serving God as a master. You cannot serve two masters; or you will love one and hate the other. Remember what Jesus told the Pharisee's when they asked him if he did his works through the devil. Jesus told them you cannot give honor to one while lifting the other. So, we have all these different religious beliefs, but if they preach the message of Jesus Christ then they are all serving the same master. Why do you think Jesus warned us how to test for false prophets? In my opinion he knew there was a time coming when there would be a lot of different religious beliefs and he wanted us to be able to tell which ones where serving God as the master and which one was serving Satan as the master. Satan will attempt to mirror everything God has that includes religion as well. The test is do they preach the death, burial, and resurrection? If they preach that they are serving the same master which is Jesus Christ even if they have some other beliefs on how a Christian should live and worship. If we can see that and come together, we will then be ready for the Great Revival. Of course, it will happen with us or without us, because it has been spoken by God. I know we all think that we are doing everything we can to spread our message and belief across the world and it is a good thing, and we are part of the great revival. But I want you to imagine if we were all joined in one accord it would be a move like in the upper room. That would shake this world and make Satan tremble. I do not want someone reading this to think I am talking about a one world religion. That is far from what I am talking about. Trust me when I say when the antichrist rules and gets his one world religion it will not be a religion that preaches the death, burial, and resurrection.

Endnote

I t has been a long journey to accomplish what God asked me to do. I set out to accomplish this task almost three years ago and I am trusting God to do something with it. I can only guess that the reason God moved me back to Kentucky is so that I would attend a different church and be able to look at this without prejudice. I can only hope you will see the message of The Two Promises for what it truly is trying to do and that is to bring different religious beliefs together to unite and act as one to get the message across this world. It is time to put our differences aside and line up together as one army for the Lord Jesus Christ.

I feel the stories from the Left Behind series were on to something and showed good people who got left behind but never gave a reason for them being left out of the Rapture. The Two Promises I feel can shed light on their story and the questions I would ask everyone reading this book is:

1. Do you feel you have served your God well enough to make the rapture?

2. If you say yes, how would you feel if you knew the Rapture happened and you missed it?

I fear too many people would make a bad choice if they knew they missed the Rapture. If you understood the Two Promises, then you would know you still have hope of eternal life. This means do not pledge allegiance to the beast and be prepared to die for Christ if necessary. It will be a very difficult time, but you still have the second promise. As I presented in the question of who will be on earth during the 1000-year millennium it was answered in Revelation chapter 20. The scriptures say the souls of those that were beheaded for the witness of Jesus and the Word which is those that were raptured. That scripture also says those that had not worshipped the beast, neither his image, or had received his mark upon their foreheads, or in their hands which are the living people from all nations after Armageddon. Yes, this could be controversial but please study and pray for God to open your eyes.